BRUSH YOUR TEETH

DROOLEY KISSES

Published by Drooley Kisses

Billy Rae did not like to brush her teeth.

Her Mama would say, "Brush your teeth, Billy Rae."

Her Papa would say, "Brush your teeth twice a day."

Billy Rae would hop up and down and shout, "But I don't want to brush my teeth every day!"

Billy Rae was mighty fond of doughnuts.
She munched on chips.

She liked to eat marshmallows with chocolate dips.

But Billy Rae did not want to brush her teeth.

Her Granny would say, "Brush your teeth Billy Rae, or they will rot and decay."

Billy Rae flashed a smile in the mirror. "They look white and bright as daylight!"

Her Grandpa would say, "They won't always stay bright if you don't brush them right!"

Billy Rae gulped down a few candies, bars of chocolate, and drank from a juice box.

"I will brush my teeth every now and then," she conceded.

"But I will decide how and when!"

So, once every few days, Billy Rae brushed her teeth in all the wrong ways.

Until one bright sunny day.

When the whole neighborhood heard Billy Rae's shout of dismay.

"My teeth have dark spots!" she cried.

"I told you to brush your teeth every day, didn't I?" Mama replied.

"My teeth look ugly!" she cried unhappily.

"You wouldn't listen to us, Billy Rae," said Granny with pity.

"What do I do now?" asked Billy Rae.

"You brush your teeth twice a day. Let me show you how," said Papa.

Papa and Billy Rae grabbed their toothbrushes.

They squirted a dollop of toothpaste on them.

"Now watch me brush my teeth just right," said Papa.

They brushed their teeth up and down.

They brushed their teeth back and forth.

They brushed their teeth from side to side.

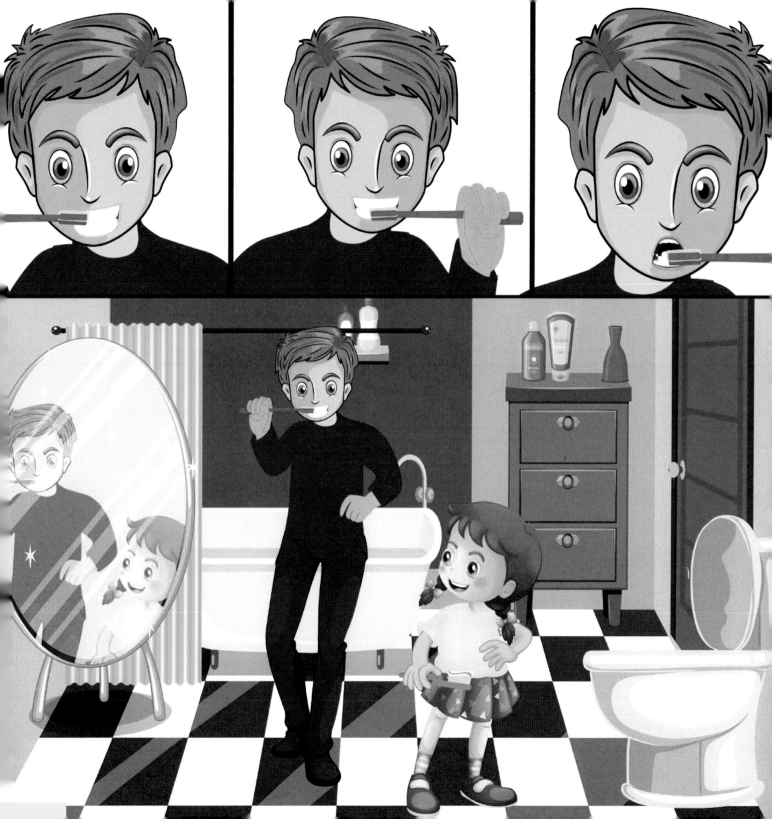

When Billy Rae smiled in the mirror, she was surprised.

Her spots were gone after brushing her teeth just right.

They were sparkling clean and bright!

Billy Rae learned to brush her teeth twice a day.

Her teeth shone bright white that way!

THE END